INTRODUCTION

Instagram has become one of the most popular social media platforms in the world, with over one billion active users. As a result, Instagram has become a powerful tool for individuals and businesses to showcase their content and reach a wider audience. Instagram content creation has become increasingly important, as it is a key factor in attracting followers, building brand awareness, and increasing engagement. Creating high-quality, visually appealing content that resonates with your audience is essential for success on Instagram. In this digital age, Instagram content creation has become an art form and requires a combination of creativity, strategy, and technical skills to stand out in a crowded social media landscape. Whether you are an individual or a brand, mastering Instagram content creation is crucial to achieving your goals on the platform.

INSTAGRAM CONTENT CREATION

Instagram has become one of the most popular social media platforms today, and it is no secret that creating engaging and visually appealing content is key to growing a following and increasing engagement. Here are some tips for creating effective Instagram content:

1. Know your audience: Understanding your target audience is essential in creating content that resonates with them. Research their interests, demographics, and preferences to tailor your content to their needs.

2. Develop a Theme: Establishing a consistent theme for your content will make your account stand out. This can be achieved through a specific color palette, a particular style of photography, or a common subject matter.

3. Use High-Quality Visuals: Instagram is a visual platform, so it is crucial to use high-quality visuals that are engaging and eye-catching. Invest in a good camera or use photo editing apps to enhance your images.

4. Be Creative with Captions: Captions are an opportunity to connect with your audience and showcase your brand's personality. Be creative, witty, and engaging in your captions while keeping them concise and to the point.

5. Post Consistently: Consistency is the key on Instagram, and it's essential to maintain a

regular posting schedule to keep your audience engaged. Plan your content in advance and use scheduling tools to post at optimal times.

6. Utilize Hashtags: Hashtags are a powerful tool to increase your reach and get your content in front of new audiences. Use relevant and trending hashtags to expand your reach and gain more followers.

7. Engage with Your Audience: Engagement is critical on Instagram, and it's essential to respond to comments and messages promptly. Use Instagram's features like polls and questions to encourage engagement and interaction with your audience.

In conclusion, creating engaging and visually appealing content is essential to grow your Instagram following and increase engagement. By understanding your audience, developing a theme, using high-quality visuals, being creative with captions, posting consistently, utilizing hashtags, and engaging with your audience, you can create a successful Instagram content strategy.

How to film for high quality

Filming high-quality video requires a combination of technical skill, creativity, and attention to detail. Whether you're a professional filmmaker or just getting started with video production, there are some basic principles that can help you achieve the best possible results. Here are some tips on how to film for high quality:

1. Plan your shots. Before you start filming, it's important to have a clear idea of what you want to capture. This means planning your shots in advance and thinking about how you want to frame your subject. Take the time to visualize your shots and consider the composition, lighting, and camera angle.

2. Use good lighting. Lighting is one of the most important factors in creating a high-quality video. If possible, try to shoot in natural light or use professional lighting equipment to create the right atmosphere for your scene. Avoid shooting in low-light conditions, as this can result in grainy footage that is difficult to edit.

3. Use a tripod. A steady camera is essential for high-quality video. A tripod can help you

achieve a smooth, stable shot, even when you're moving around. Invest in a good-quality tripod that can support your camera and provide the stability you need for your shots.

4. Choose the right camera settings. Your camera settings can have a big impact on the quality of your footage. Choose the right resolution and frame rate for your project, and adjust your exposure and white balance to ensure that your shots are well-lit and properly balanced.

5. Use good audio equipment. Good sound is just as important as good video. Invest in a quality microphone to capture clear, crisp audio. Consider using a boom mic or lapel mic to capture sound from your subject, and

use headphones to monitor your audio while you're filming.

6. Use a variety of shots and angles. Variety is key when it comes to creating engaging videos. Use a variety of shots and cameras.

7. Plan Your Videos in Advance. Poor technique isn't the only thing that can make a video look unprofessional. A lack of planning can also leave viewers underwhelmed with your finished product. By taking the time to plan your video thoroughly before you start production, you can ensure that the quality of your actual content is just as good as the quality of your footage.

8.   Shoot from a variety of angles. Cutting from one angle to another is a good (and simple) way to add visual interest to your professional videos. This is an especially useful technique if you're making a how-to video, a product demo, or another type of video that shows you doing something rather than just talking.

9.   Work On Your Camera Presence. If you appear in your professional videos, the way you carry yourself on camera has an enormous impact on how professional your content looks. Appearing nervous, fidgety, or uncomfortable on camera will distract viewers from your message.

10.   Use your phone the right way. No DSLR camera? No problem. You can use your phone

to keep capture professional video footage – the quality is just fine for most purposes. But there are a few things in mind if you're going to use your phone for video creation. Use the camera on the back of your phone. The front camera's quality is not as good on most phones. Record in landscape mode (that is, horizontally instead of vertically). This will give you footage that looks good on larger devices, not just phone screens. If your phone has a feature that allows you to overlay a grid on your screen, use it. This will help you keep your phone level and avoid tilted footage.

11.   Understand the Rule of Thirds. The rule of thirds is one of the most basic principles of film composition. Imagine that there's a 3-by-3 grid laid over the field you're filming. Instead

of placing your subject right in the middle of the shot, you should place your subject along one of the lines of the grid. The points where the lines intersect are particularly strong areas of focus, so situate important elements of the video there if you can.

12. Avoid shaky footage. Shaky footage will make any professional video look like a home movie (and it can make your viewers feel seasick, to boot). It's hard to hold a camera completely steady, so try not to hold your camera at all if you can help it. Instead, use a tripod or set your camera on a sturdy surface. Once you've got your camera set up, try not to move it unless you have to. Panning around constantly detracts from the professional look of a video. Rather than moving the camera if you have to change perspective, it's better to cut from one shot to another. If your footage turns out shaky despite your best efforts, video stabilization software can help fix it afterwards. Some cameras also have built-in stabilization that you can use while you're filming. Slowing down your footage can also help to make shakiness less obvious.

13. Prioritize crisp, clear audio. Your audio quality is actually more important than your professional video quality. Most people are willing to watch a video that's not shot in HD or that's even a little grainy, as long as everything else about it is good. But fuzzy, indistinct audio is usually enough to make anyone hit the "back" button within a few seconds of starting to play a video. Because audio matters so much, a good microphone is the first piece of equipment you should invest in. Get the best one you can afford. For $100 to $200, you can get a microphone that performs well and will last a long time. There are also some decent options under $100 if you're on a tight budget. Even I will do it! Capture clear audio by putting your microphone as close to the subject as possible. You might want to use a pop filter to eliminate blips and crackles on the finished recording. Be aware of any background noise that your microphone might be picking up, too. It's easy to tune out things like traffic, birds, and even the noise of the wind, but all of these sounds will be very obvious on your recording.

14. Use a clean background. Be deliberate about the background you use for filming. Nothing looks less professional than a messy or distracting background. One easy way to get a

professional look for your video is to use a solid-colored background. A wall, a bed sheet, or a large sheet of backdrop paper is all good options. Make sure your subject stands several feet away from the backdrop to avoid casting shadows on it. It's also a good idea to shoot a video in a "professional" environment—the place where you actually work or spend time. For instance, makes her professional videos in her home office. Make sure to check out this video for both a great example of a filming set and some great tips on how to actually set up a home office. Be careful not to film with a window or another reflective surface in the background of your shot. You could inadvertently catch the camera in the reflection. Besides that, having a light source like a window behind your subject can make the subject look dark and shadowy.

15. Tell a story. One of the main reasons viewers lose interest in a video is a lack of storytelling. A single image or a short video clip can make a profound statement, relay a witty anecdote, or make a poignant observation on the human condition. Change your focus from one subject to another or build drama with interesting lighting; the choices are up to you. Build emotion into the story and keep the viewer's attention. Choose a premise that people can relate to. Add a bit of conflict, and finally conclude with some kind of resolution. These are all basic elements of story-telling, but it's up to you to decide how to present them within the context of your own unique vision. You must also consider the demographics of your audience. Who are you making the video

for? For example, are you making a commercial for a fast-food chain or for a clothing brand?

16.   Improve Your Composition.   A professional filmmaker or someone from the motion picture industry may be able to spot the work of an amateur during the first few seconds of a video project. That's still true even if high-end camera equipment was used. So what gives them away? It's their lack of proper framing and composition. What many beginners don't realize is that good videographer (especially cinematography) involves more than just aiming your camera at your scene or subject. It involves arranging and allowing visual elements to tell your story. It also means changing your camera's framing in order to make the scene look aesthetically pleasing. Among the most important cinematic

videography tips and compositional rules, this is where you place your subject's head a little higher (not at the center) of the frame and give them visual breathing or walking space when facing the sides. Another is to remain on the same side of two people talking when taking over-the-shoulder shots. Also, having a foreground and a background to create depth within a scene is crucial.

17.   Set your white balance. A real challenge that many professionals go through is temperature and color correction. If you're using more than one camera to record the same scene, it's possible for the cameras to have different default color temperatures. This is an issue when using cameras from different brands, like Sony and Canon. It can also be a

problem when using cameras from the same brand. Can you imagine how distracting it would be to see alternating bluish and warm yellow clips? Set the white balance on all cameras before recording to produce more consistent, professional-looking clips. This will help speed up the editing process and reduce post-production costs in the future. Bonus Tip: The "correct" white balance is subjective and can depend on your desired output. For example, you could intentionally set it to look even colder to give the scene a more chilly or scary vibe. Use it to work for your story, as long as you practice consistency in each unique scene.

How to edit on Vlog now

Blogging has become one of the most popular forms of content creation in recent years. With the rise of social media platforms like YouTube and Instagram, more and more people are turning to vlogging to share their lives and experiences with the world. However, for many aspiring vloggers, the editing process can be daunting. Editing is an essential part of the vlogging process, as it helps to create a polished and professional-looking final product. In this article, we will discuss how to edit on "Vlog Now," popular editing software for vloggers.

Step 1: Import your footage

The first step in editing your vlog on "Vlog Now" is to import your footage. This can be done by simply dragging and dropping your files into the software. Once your footage is imported, you can arrange it in the order that you want it to appear in your final video.

Step 2: Trim and cut your footage

After importing your footage, the next step is to trim and cut your footage. This involves removing any unwanted footage, such as awkward pauses or mistakes. "Vlog Now" makes this process easy by allowing you to select the section of your footage that you want to remove and then pressing the delete key.

Step 3: Add transitions and effects

Adding transitions and effects can help to make your vlog more visually appealing and engaging. "Vlog Now" comes with a variety of transitions and effects that you can use to enhance your video. Some popular options include cross fades, fades to black and slow-motion effects.

Step 4: Add music and sound effects

Music and sound effects can also help to enhance your vlog and create a more immersive experience for your viewers. "Vlog Now" allow you to easily add music and sound effects to your video. You can either choose from the software's built-in library or import your own audio files.

Step 5: Color grading

Color grading is the process of adjusting the colors in your video to create a more cinematic look. "Vlog Now" comes with a variety of color grading tools that allow you to adjust the brightness, contrast, and saturation of your footage. You can also add filters to give your video a specific look and feel.

Step 6: Export your video

Once you have finished editing your vlog, the final step is to export your video. "Vlog Now" makes this process easy by allowing you to select the format and resolution of your video. You can also choose to export your video in different aspect ratios, depending on where you plan to publish it.

In conclusion, editing your vlog on "Vlog Now" is a simple and straightforward process. By following these six steps, you can create a polished and professional-looking video that will engage and entertain your viewers. Whether you are a seasoned vlogger or just starting out, "Vlog Now" is powerful editing software that can help you take your vlogs to the next level.

Step 7: Develop your vlog niche.

Before you start filming your vlog, it's important to figure out whom you're filming for and what viewers will be interested in your vlog content. Decide on a target audience and create videos that will add value to the lives of those watching them. From cooking segments to home decor, makeup tutorials, gaming, fitness, and a cleaning time-lapse, there's a vlog for every audience Make sure you're passionate about the topic you choose, so your audience will be too.

Commences

Step 8: Determine your vlog story.

Creators should establish what is going to be featured in the vlog before filming commences. If there is no clear plan on what is going to be recorded, the vlog might turn out muddled and messy, and editing is going to take a lot longer than expected.

While a vlog might be in the "day in the life" style, creators should still plan what to record and how to record it to make it more interesting. Like recording a time-lapse, montage, overhead shots, or with a voiceover, beginning, middle, and end Planned content with a beginning, middle, and end generally results in a more successful vlog. Develop an idea and a general sense of how a story will unfold from it. Think of your vlog like a best-selling novel. An interesting premise will hook viewers and lead them to subscribe to your YouTube channel roll

Step 9: Plan of action.

Start your vlog off with a pen and paper, or pull up the Notes app on your Smartphone. Begin by writing down your story ideas that you've just created, and then pair segments with how you will show them visually. Shooting roll can add extra value to your vlog with little effort. Creating a rough outline with key points and visuals might just take your vlog to the next level. Ideally, record your vlog in chronological order so that when you upload your footage to Clip champ, you don't have to rearrange the clips on the timeline. Once you've edited a few vlogs, don't be shy about changing up your vlog format throughout the week.

Personal Mistakes (Mistakes)

- Have a Strategy: You are need to go in with a strategy in mind. Because there are millions of other influencers out there, you need to demonstrate to users why you are unique and what sets apart the quality of your content from that of other influencers. Establishing a "personality" for your account requires adhering to a predetermined approach and developing powerful brand identification. You may also set goals for yourself by planning, and these goals can be based on the content of your page; for example, are you hoping to make money from it? Increasing your sales is the next logical step for you to take.

Are you attempting to make people more aware of something? Concentrate on growing the number of people who follow you. When you go into a situation with a clear plan, it is much simpler to handle it, track it, and make progress.

- Forget Irrelevant Content: After you have established who you are, the worst thing that you could do for yourself would be to post content that has absolutely nothing to do with your image.

Instagram users will occasionally publish content that is currently popular in order to quickly attract followers, even if the content in question has nothing to do with the rest of their posts. Don't make the same mistake as them. It lessens the impact of your actual brand and may cause you to lose followers if they get the impression that you are disorganized or, even worse, viral...

- Be Astute Regarding the Use of Hashtags: Hashtags are an excellent tool for putting your articles on the map, gaining you more visibility, and streamlining the content you share, as you surely already know. But are you utilizing them to their full potential? Learn to avoid using basic ones such as #girl because there are probably millions of posts like that and yours is likely to get buried in the noise of all the other similar posts. Make sure that the hashtags you use are relevant to the content of your post. Consider which other topics you would like to be related with, and give some thought to how you might maintain a consistent theme throughout your photographs.

- Commenting in a Spammy Manner: Avoid Doing It When we talk about commenting in a spammy manner, we are not referring to the comments that your followers leave on your posts (although you may wish to delete those). Instead, we are talking about the comments that YOU leave. This includes your reactions to other people's posts, your captions, and your comments on your own posts.

If you publish broken links or make comments that are generic or spammy like "Hey, check out my page...", it is likely that you will leave your followers (and possibly even other users) feeling a bit angry. Make sure that your virtual assistant or social media manager is engaging in genuine conversation with other users if they are managing your account on your behalf. This is especially important if they are managing your account on social media. Keep in mind that every interaction you (or your account) has with other users on Instagram will be interpreted as a reflection of both you and your account.

- Keep in Mind the Importance of Direct Messages: You have our permission to approach decision makers in companies, so be ready to make some noise! Direct Messages provide you with the option to communicate with brands about the possibility of working together, and if they are interested, they can quickly browse your profile to learn more about you and your work. Additionally, it is a form of contact that is a great deal more immediate; nobody enjoys having to respond to a plethora of emails.

You can also communicate privately with a subset of your followers by using direct messages (DMs). This would lend a more personal touch to your fans, and it would also benefit you to inquire as to the kind of content they already enjoy, as well as the types of content they would like to see in the future.

5 Ways to Turn Your Mistake into a Valuable Life Lesson

1. Acknowledge your errors. So often, leaders say things like, "I'm sorry you felt that way," or "It's unfortunate it didn't work out." But blaming other people or minimizing your responsibility isn't helpful to anyone.

Before you can learn from your mistakes, you have to accept full responsibility for your role in the outcome. That can be uncomfortable sometimes, but until you can say, "I messed up," you aren't ready to change.

2. Ask yourself tough questions. While you don't want to dwell on your mistakes, reflecting on them can be productive. Ask yourself a few tough questions:

• What went wrong?

- What could I do better next time?
- What did I learn from this?

Write down your responses and you'll see the situation a little more clearly. Seeing your answers on paper can help you think more logically about an irrational or emotional experience.

3. Make a plan. Beating yourself up for your mistakes won't help you down the road. It's important to spend the bulk of your time thinking about how to do better in the future. Make a plan that will help you avoid making a similar mistake. Be as detailed as possible, but remain flexible since your plan may need to change.

Whether you find accountability partner or track your progress on a calendar, find a way to hold yourself accountable. Keep in mind that what works for one person might not work for someone else.

4. Make it harder to mess up. Don't depend on willpower alone to prevent you from taking an unhealthy shortcut or from giving into immediate gratification. Increase your chances of success by making it harder to mess up again.

5. Create a List of Reasons Why YouDon't Want to Make the Mistake Again Sometimes; it only takes one weak moment to indulge in something you shouldn't. Creating a list of all the reasons why you should stay on track could help you stay self-disciplined, even during the toughest times.

How I reached 90k followers within three month

Gaining 90,000 followers in just three months is a remarkable feat and requires a lot of hard work, dedication, and strategic planning. Here are some potential factors that may have contributed to your success:

1. Consistency: Posting consistently is key to building a following on social media. By consistently sharing high-quality content that resonates with your target audience, you establish trust and build a loyal following. You may have found a schedule that worked well for you, such as posting daily or multiple times a week that will helped you reach 90,000 followers quickly.

2. Engaging content: Creating content that is interesting, informative, or entertaining can help attract and retain followers. Your content may have stood out from others in your niche, making it more likely for people to follow and engage with you. Additionally,

responding to comments and messages promptly can help build a community around your brand and foster deeper connections with your followers.

3. Niche focus: By focusing on a specific niche or topic, you may have attracted a dedicated following that is interested in your content. Being known as an expert or authority in a particular area can help you stand out in a crowded social media landscape.

4. Collaboration: Collaborating with other influencers or brands in your niche can help you reach a wider audience and gain new followers. By partnering with others to create content or cross-promote each other's accounts, you may have been able to reach

more people and increase your visibility.

5. Paid advertising: Investing in paid advertising can help you reach a larger audience and attract new followers. By targeting your ads to specific demographics or interests, you may have been able to attract followers who are more likely to be interested in your content.

It's important to note that there is no one-size-fits-all approach to gaining followers on social media. What works for one person may not work for another, and success often requires experimentation and adaptability. However, by focusing on creating engaging content, building a strong community, and staying true to your brand, you can continue to grow your following and achieve your social media goals.

IMPORTANT TIPS

• Create a lot of content ahead of time so you can post consistently and have more options.

• Distinguish between artistic and non-aesthetic shots

• Instead of setting end objectives, set output goals. For example, instead of setting a goal of 100k followers set a target of making 1000 videos in one year.

• Don't wait for the right time to start; you'll learn by doing."It is preferable to begin incorrectly in order to pause perfectly.

• I film in 4k/30fps on my iPhone and export it to "vlog now" with the same settings (4k/30fps).

• Instagram quality button: "turn on" to upload at the highest quality.

Motivational for someone who wants to reach 90,000 followers within three months

Here's a motivational message for you:

I understand that you have set a goal for yourself to reach 90,000 followers within three months on Instagram through your content creation. It's a challenging goal, but not impossible to achieve with hard work, dedication, and strategic planning. Remember that the key to success is not just the numbers, but also the quality of the content that you create. Focus on producing content that is engaging, inspiring, and resonates with your target audience. Make sure to be consistent in your posting and maintain a regular schedule to keep your followers engaged.

It's also important to keep up with the latest trends and best practices in your niche. Research your competitors and see what they are doing to attract and engage their audience. Take inspiration from their work, but also try to bring your unique perspective and style to your content.

Engagement is crucial to growing your following, so make sure to respond to comments, messages, and DMs regularly. Engage with other users in your niche by commenting on and liking their posts. Collaborate with other creators to reach a wider audience and cross-promote each other's accounts. In addition to your regular content, consider creating and promoting Instagram stories and reels. These formats are becoming increasingly popular on the platform and can help you gain more visibility and attract new followers.

Finally, don't be afraid to invest in paid advertising to reach a larger audience. With Instagram's targeting options, you can reach specific demographics and interests to attract new followers who are likely to be interested in your content.

Remember that reaching your goal requires hard work, dedication, and persistence. Don't give up if you don't see immediate results, keep pushing yourself to create better content, engage with your followers, and try new strategies.

Believe in yourself and your abilities, and stay focused on your goal. With determination and a willingness to learn and adapt, you can achieve anything you set your mind to. I have no doubt that you have what it takes to reach 90,000 followers within three months through your content creation on Instagram. Keep pushing yourself, stay motivated, and always remember that the journey to success is just as important as the destination.

www.ingramcontent.com/pod-product-compliance
Lightning Source LLC
Chambersburg PA
CBHW070336240526
45466CB00027B/2106